The City Cat and the Country Cat

Written by Anne Miranda
Illustrated by Deborah Melmon

A city cat went to
see a country cat.

3

"What can we do here?"
asked the city cat.
"We can camp,"
said the country cat.

4

The city cat did not
like to camp.

"We can dance in a circle,"
said the country cat.

The city cat did not like to dance in a circle.

The city cat did not
like the country.

"Come home with me,"
said the city cat.

"What can we do here?"
asked the country cat.

"We can ride in a cab,"
said the city cat.

The country cat did not like to ride in a cab.

"What can we do here?" asked the country cat.

"We can go to the circus,"
said the city cat.

13

The country cat did
not like the circus.

The country cat did
not like the city.
The city cat did not
like the country.

15